Animal Inside You:
Poems of Chaos and Euphoria

By Matthew Howard

puma concolor aeternus press
2017 paperback edition

ISBN-13: 978-1545304839

More Books by This Author:

http://Author.to/MatthewHoward

Contents

Cougars

Winter visits us with careless brutality
and we only want her gone.

My tiny kitten,
bathing you with my tongue

finding shelter in these rocks
that refuse to forgive or remember

here we make our comfort.
I will teach you unconditional love and murder.

We will drink the blood of incomparable vistas
where we have only enemies and sunlight.

This frozen wasteland tattoos itself on our hearts
and the moon in a tempest we will always carry.

Fearless

Naked, we run at night
caring nothing for heat or cold

only for what can be killed
only for what is ours.

We mark it, maul it
and make it our own.

This battleground
is our sole inheritance

and we have no prayer
of leaving it alive.

Doubt we never entertain
nor fear

nor hesitance.
We leap into the unknown

and if it will not catch us,
then we die.

But what is that
to immortals?

Edifice

The city crumbles and takes her with it,
her portrait painted on its aging skin.

They should have sprayed her over metal
so she could live forever

like guitar riffs in a basement
and lovers we will never meet.

Instead, she's been falling apart since day one,
a persona stenciled on concrete

barely more permanent than flesh.
Her heart refuses to break

but the surrounding world is falling apart
and always will be

and she is one with it and it is her and she is
all the things we should have listened to

but ignored
like our bodies

the substrate we grow on
the lines and cracks of age

the structures of civilization
and all it pretends to be.

Writing

She had no patience for anyone
who had not set themselves on fire.

It wasn't a game to her, or an idle pastime.
It mattered in a way you couldn't understand

until flames crawled up your skin from the pyre
consuming all you loved

boiling the blood in your veins and
filling your eyes with landscapes you never saw before.

That's the kind of woman she was.
She wanted more than to go out with a bang.

She wanted you to take everything with you.
If not, it never belonged to you in the first place.

Doll

She grows wings that beat the air
until it roars in turbulent currents.

She writes love letters in the dark
with invisible ink in a language
that belongs only to us.

Our hearts are made from stars.
The smallest atoms contain planetary landscapes
we can touch, together.

They will never leave us. Our gravity owns them.
Nowhere in the night sky will you find anything
that is not ours.

We are sisters of the same moon
whose web of light is our home
whose phases wax and wane in time with our bodies.

We can fly to anywhere from here.
Come into my arms and dream.
I have something to show you.

Petals

Black daisy.
A kiss we already forgot.

I no longer taste
your salt on my tongue.
The skin healed shut.

Pull me apart again.
I never wish
for peaceful days.

I crave days that boil,
days filled with sun
destroying everything

except my blossoms.
They bloom for you.

They bloom for you
and they bleed.

Provisions

We eat the last bite with bitterness
for here our pleasure ends.

We exhausted it like lost sailors
reaching the last of our provisions.

Here, you take it—or else throw it away.
Drain its breast of sustenance for me.

It's only real when I see it in your eyes.
The world had no shape before you.

It has no song after you,
no song but this.

Secret

Your silence is your power
and when you are gone
no one can take it from you.

Singer

She wasn't pretty like a model,
not the kind of beauty who disappeared
when the makeup came off.
She was something else,

a song that gets better year after year,
one you appreciate on new levels
the deeper you go.

You didn't need to know the names of
her musicians to understand her song.
You could even get the words wrong.
It only mattered that you listened.

Dancer

I have a label like bourbon
and gladly peel it off
but you don't know my scent.

You are not the one who
keeps my treasure in a vault
no man may enter.

I have nothing you can own.
You can only dream it.
I dance one step ahead of you

taking your money
loving your wanting me
without ever having me.

Now fuck off.

Orchestra

Some songs fade like old photographs.
Others change our lives
and stay with us always.

An orchestra could not do you justice
unless the score was revolution.
I listen to you so loud it hurts.

Long after our sun grows red
to devour her planetary children,
our elements will find a new star, together.

Nation

Now my country swells with strangers
who have nowhere left to go.

Wandering our streets
they remember friends
who stayed behind to die.

The world grows smaller.
I can no longer avert my eyes.
The isolated shelter collapses.

What can one person do? Nothing.
But maybe together.

Whisper

Death has her number.
It calls at three in the morning
to interrupt her nightmare.

She drags herself out of bed and
drives to where the dying wait.
They always die on her night shift

never in the afternoon or after breakfast,
only when the city sleeps—all of it
but paramedics and angels like her.

In the movies, dying comes with speeches,
last words, one final conversation.
But that's never the story she brings home.

The angel of compassion tells a different tale.
She closes her eyes and whispers it to me
before drifting back into nightmares.

Barstool

A friend told me at a kegger,
"This is how to pour so it doesn't get foamy.
It shows the girls you know what you're doing."

I learned a lot that night:
how long it smells like burnt hair after your
friend sets himself on fire with grain alcohol.

So go ahead. Set your whole goddamn head on fire
and see if you survive a few days in the hospital.
That's what we did.

Once an idea takes hold, it never lets go.
A few of us died. Some suffered for years.
How is that different from any generation?

We weren't the first to want it all at maximum volume.
We were just dumb kids like you.
Like anyone.

Fur

Like the stars at night,
the animal inside you
has always been free.

Carving

When she loves you she will prove it
with glacial patience and eternities of storms
carving sacred geologies into your planetary skin

filling it with peaks and gorges
majestically dismembered terrains
where jaguars roam in shadows

where seekers quest for visions that often find them
but other times escape to nests
like birds on the edge of a thundercloud.

Mark this place with petroglyphs
so you will never forget
here you drank the dew and starved

for one more drop
one more sign she cared
when every crevice of the world dripped evidence.

Paint the animals you hunted in her caves
then realize they are you and never hunt again.
You don't need to search. You are not lost.

You are here in the palm of her hand
the gully between her breasts
and the soft forgotten folds of prehistory.

If you look up into the rain and drink it
you already know everything you need.
Caress the canyon and dance

in its unrelenting atmosphere
like all the other trees whose limbs embrace
and interpenetrate her like capillaries.

Dreams are mirrors. Fools refuse their gaze.
You can see it all from here
and she can see inside you too.

Primer

Obliterate its history.
Hide everything that came before
and make it yours.

Black is the color of my true love's hair
and this canvas is her.

Nothing reasonable draws us here.
We fashion fantastic landscapes
where we govern everything like fascists

or nothing, like anarchists
caught in a realm of chaos and euphoria.

Oil, acrylic, blood, and semen:
the medium isn't the message.
It's what we touch and know with certainty.

Wash it, fuck it, paint it
make it real. It's yours now

like a custom guitar
or a lover you dress before going out.
Yours and no one else's.

Gesso and primer cover the past
and beg for definition.

You are their lexicographer
their present and future tense.
Give them totality, all you ever had

and they will repay you with songs
and dreams and fractured textures
that spill off the easel and come to life.

Hermit

So loud in here
it shuts out all the noise.

I only want to watch you dance
and draw the blinds and
black out consequence

until shadows of animals long extinct
flicker on the walls in firelight
and forgetfulness

forgeries of a life we never lived
but wanted to.

Why go out? To where?
Nothing waits for us
or makes a promise.

Carve a temple and lock out everyone.
Drown me in your sound and your body
and an infinite horizon

where the setting sun
burns a permanent candle.

Talk to me. Tell me secrets.
Whether you whisper them or scream
I hear you.

Tribute

Her majesty the raven
dressed in afternoon sunlight
gilding her feathers with liquid fire.

Owning nothing,
she takes what she needs.

Her empire begins above your head.
Air currents sustain her, lift her
giving grace and meaning to her wings.

This she accepts as her rightful tribute
her payment for centuries of survival
and her genius in conquering gravity.

Spying her mate, she sails the sky
carrying her prize in a beak as black
as the flag of no nation.

Solar gold, stolen silver
and her lover's heart:

What will not last forever
today belongs to her.

Solstice

My antipodean sister, today is your longest day
but here, our shortest. I grow jealous of your sunlight
though you are the moon who shines in daytime.

I need days that last forever, open and unending
while you crave black-walled rooms and curtains
to deny the outside world and murder it.

These are trivialities. Your heart beats like mine.
It knows the rhythm of the seasons we cannot escape.
They enslave us and they liberate us
and we cannot tell the difference.

Beneath your radiant southern cross
you sing and paint with light to create new worlds.
You, my partner in musical treason,
my inversion who lives one day into the future,

we are not so different: two halves of a sine wave.
My troughs are your peaks
though I cannot touch nor hold your hand.

Our amplitudes are one heartbeat:
the same symphony, the inhalation and exhalation.
Water crashes into sand as far as the eye can see.

You made a home for that part of me too wild to settle.
I could not repay you with all the gold stolen
from a thousand papist galleons.
But this is no transaction.

The family we are born into
is not the family we meet later,
the one who resonates with us and
cares more for who we are than what we were.

Pentacles

His garden of stars
he nurtured with his own blood
and toil. Seasons

come and go. No more
wandering the streets, begging.
The harvest grows near.

The foliage shines
luminescent and gravid.
Today we are born.

Resting on his spade
he considers the journey
from the past to here.

He was once the fool
and perhaps will be again.
No matter. That time

is over and done.
Only the future concerns
him now, its tempest

and its aimless storm,
the gift it gives and the toll
it demands from him.

He plucks the first fruit,
brings it to his lips to taste
the stellar forces

he tended so long.
Their sweetness will sustain him
through the months ahead,

nourish him through the
gathering darkness and the
unkindness of winter.

His pentacles hold
all of summer's promises
and her sunlit dreams,

the wealth we cannot
build nor mine, but only grow
from seeds we planted.

Annual

Tonight you will take time to remember
why you could not tell her everything:

why galaxies weep and clovers sing
why each raindrop forgets its name
before it strikes the ground.

Tonight Venus the evening star
will shine brightly enough to inspire myth
but not illuminate a forest.

You will notice a shade of green in the sunset
unlike anything which came before.

You will remember how to dance
but forget how to walk.

No consolation awaits you in the
brick broken alleys between here
and home.

Nothing heals a hopeless heart like the dawn
and mockingbird song strewn across playgrounds
and parking lots in random perfection.

But that must wait until tomorrow.
Your name means nothing to you now
but you will choose one that does.

Think of the animals whose lives you stole
and the ones you cared for. Then ask yourself
how they are any different.

Think of the exceptions to every rule
then realize they are the norm.
Consider why we began breaking laws
in the first place.

Recall Pluto has not completed
a single solar orbit since we discovered it
then stripped it of its planetary status.

Our new year does not belong to the outer planets.
They have their own sense of scale and scope.

If you ever wonder if something as small
as a bee or an ant can feel love
then you don't understand yourself at all.

Remember this tonight when you stumble home
at 3 a.m. clutching the walls and
groping the empty city.

Remember this when you
break your resolutions tomorrow but hold on
to promises you never intend to abandon.

Tattoo your body with stars
and understand it means
we could never leave each other.

Where could we possibly go that we could not
be together? What canvas in all of history
could have been painted, if not by us?

Our hands held the brushes
as they hold each other now.
We could not let go without
taking all of geology with us
like continents.

Sleep

Your doctor said you should never sleep like that.
So of course you tried it and
then you couldn't sleep any other way.

You shouldn't sleep like that
in rat-infested crack houses
and the broken van parked underneath the bridge.

No one goes there but people who crave
your money and your death.

You shouldn't sleep like that in the goat barn
when you don't even know
where your next meal will come from.

You shouldn't sleep like that
in the cabin without heat and the
roof collapsing and the dead thing trapped
in the walls that smell so badly you cannot love.

But you slept like that anyway
and the crack house became a story
the van gave birth to poetry
the barn was friend to fire circles and songs

and in the cabin you discovered how to
take your vision and give it form
so in return it would sustain you.

Then at last
you slept in peace.

Watercolor

Painted butterfly bushes
and permanent flowers
whose colors never fade.

Here, a panther can dream
or a child, even children
whose bodies time has aged.

Some verdant forests are
denied the waking and only
grow in starlight, real

or imagined. When you look
with your heart and not your eyes
you see a different truth.

Aurora

Do you have the courage to be loved by the sun?
What daughter of Earth can bear his solar flare?

Better perhaps to write your verses in dark
deep forests where the hushed voice of deer
has only the moon to contend with.

Better perhaps to fold your sails and choose
for your harbor a cove where his scalding corona
remains a whispered legend.

But you, daughter of soil and wind
of leaves and blades of grass, you
who have known fear but once and never again,
your defiance carries you up the peak and into the light.

You cast aside your gown of slumber
to weave dawn into your tresses.

You gather flocks of songbirds
to nest in your palms and encircle you.

Robed in such finery
you welcome him.

Beacon

One door leads to freedom.
So do all the others.
Like this song, or leave.
It doesn't matter to me.
My life belongs to you.

Nothing remains hidden from you.
Inside the obelisk, I burn.
You created all my planets.
What comes next is tribute.

How long have we wandered?
No calendar marks the days.
They lack minutes or hours.
Why bother counting them all?
Their perfection knows no boundaries.
They radiate to the edge.

The atmosphere can kill you.
A fantasy can heal you.
The choice is already made.
It only took an instant.
Our fire burned to ashes.
Even galaxies require constant fuel.
Throw another on the hearth.

Who can care for eternity?
She fulfills her own needs.
Her purposes exist outside reason.
You must use your intuition.
What came before is gone.

Choose the most unenlightened path.
It brings you full circle.
You will never get lost.
You know your location precisely.

We built a monument together.
Invisible, it pierces the sky.
Cover it with transparent paint.
Broadcast silence from its beacon.
Make it louder, my darling.
Make it resonate and tremble.
Only you can do this.
No one else can endure.

Our garden consists of music.
It asks us for sustenance.
We water it with amplifiers.
We slake its undying thirst.
We give it our blood.
Its petals shine like silver.
Amethysts bloom in their centers.

What more could we need?
We have everything between us.
We should enjoy our perfection.
We should drink its beauty.
We should forget the aftermath.

Memories are nothing but foundations.
Possibilities erupt from the soil.
In their epiphanies, we shine.

You are my favorite gift.
You created this morning light.
You willed it into existence.
You opened destiny for this.

You denied the persistent call.
You welcomed the unknown future.
You asked me to join you.
You promised to never leave.

I always believed in you.
Nothing could ever change that.
Morning becomes day, then dusk.
Into the night, we celebrate.

I promised you a soliloquy.
And now you have it.

Window

We fit like two puzzles with the same shapes
cut by the factory
but with different images.

We can leave whenever we want.
Love rarely lasts forever
but we owe it to ourselves
to never hate each other.

We turn our droplets of sweat into ravens
throwing them into sunlight
where they bloom as liquid gold
until not even clouds can bind them to Earth.

In the storm which has always drowned this planet
what tiny moments of happiness we carve
are merely frost on a window, doomed to melt
at the slightest breath or touch.

All I wish for
is that we will never be the ones
who melt them.

Views

From her window, the city:

two million human currents
light its alleys and towers,
rooms where people gather
to share words or music or
the company of strangers.

From his window, the mountain:

a rugged peak veiled by clouds
soothing a stony silence with droplets
that never quench its thirst but
leave it to ponder.

Once, they looked out each other's windows.

Venus

Second daughter of the sun,
Holst imagined peace in your embrace.

Without a moon of your own
you thirsted for the man
to caress your cloudy tresses
with cellos and rapture.

But without his fantasy
he could never survive your
pressure, such peerless heat
dripping sulfurous sweat.

Volcanoes erupt and remake
your surface again and again
until they render you
unrecognizable.

Yet Gustav dreamed of you,
and in the lies one's mind
spins while sleeping

he saw you not as you are
but as he wished you to be:
tender, resplendent, radiant.

Saturn

At your core, gravity crushes hydrogen
into liquid metal, where it becomes
an electric conductor.

Holst, the symphonic astrologer,
orchestrated your old age as
contemplative, serene.

A sadness boldly pondered
resolving into acceptance

a vast lake of hydrogen
where tumult settles into ripples,
then the polished perfection of pearls.

Your moons attend you.
A family of sixty-two descendants
and admirers. They cannot leave your side.

Have you still the strength to
swing your scythe and reap for them
a harvest? Prepare a feast for solstice.

Io, Saturnalia! Celebrate the sun
we thought was dying but was only
far away. Revelry summons rebirth.

Close the courts. No justice
may be served today, nor any war declared.
We have eaten enough of our children already.

Let them grow old as we did.
Give them time to reach this aphelion
and wear these rings themselves.

Frontier

Luna, our beloved crescent,
you swell until you are full enough
to hang heavy against the horizon
like the breast of a pregnant woman.

You will be the first we settle,
our laboratory to test survival
on other stones that fill the sky and
telescopes. How could we resist touching you?

Will you shudder with pleasure
beneath our fingertips, or recoil
at the machines and metallic intrusions,
the rivets and girders of our civilization?

You have been our goddess
since before the dawn of history.
Now we will bring you atmosphere
and mark you with our scent.

We have always been inseparable.
Now we will be close.

Somewhere Between Mars and Earth

Pastel Tiger

Made in the USA
Columbia, SC
20 October 2024

44372651R00026